Facing Cancer Together

HOW TO HELP YOUR FRIEND OR LOVED ONE

Pamela N. Brown

FACING CANCER TOGETHER
How to Help Your Friend or Loved One

Cover design by Marti Naughton
Book design by Timothy W. Larson

Library of Congress Cataloging-in-Publication Data
Brown, Pamela N., 1959–
Facing cancer together: how to help your friend or loved one / Pamela N. Brown.
p. cm.
Includes bibliographical references.
ISBN 0-8066-3833-8 (alk. paper)
1. Cancer—Patients—Care. 2. Caregivers 3. Brown, Pamela N., 1959—Health. 4. Hodgkin's disease—Patients—United States Biography. I. Title
RC262.B765 1999
362.1'9699446'0092—dc 21
[B]
99-14110
CIP

The paper used in this publication meets the minimum requirements of American National Standard for Information Sciences—Permanence of Paper for Printed Library Materials, ANSI Z329.48-1984.

Manufactured in the U.S.A. AF 9-3833

03 02 01 00 99 1 2 3 4 5 6 7 8 9 10

Contents

To God
be the glory!

Foreword

Over the past several years, my wife and I have been encouraging cancer patients and amputees through Outreach of Hope, an organization we started as a result of my cancer diagnosis and ultimate amputation of my left arm and shoulder. Through this ministry, we have been privileged to meet wonderful people. Although many struggle tremendously, their lives continue to express their love for God, the offer of strength he provides and, remarkably, their desire to help others who are struggling, too.

One of these individuals I have had the privilege of meeting is Pam Brown, the author of this book. Pam has been there. She understands in a real and personal way the journey of cancer and what it takes to accompany a hurting friend or family member. Her personal experiences and work with a cancer support group she started in Colorado Springs makes her more credible than most professionals.

Beyond all this, the one thing that impressed me most about Pam is the simple fact that she has a desire to use her experience with cancer to reach out and encourage others. I believe she is living out what Paul speaks of in 2 Corinthians 1:3-5:

> Praise be to God and Father of our Lord Jesus Christ, the Father of compassion and the God of all comfort, who comforts us in all our troubles, so that we can comfort those in any trouble with the comfort we ourselves have received from God. For just as the sufferings of Christ flow over into our lives, so also through Christ our comfort overflows.

Pamela's desire is to comfort and encourage in the same way she received that comfort and encouragement from our heavenly Father.

There's a wonderful passage in the Bible where we are encouraged to love with actions and in truth. Through *Facing Cancer Together*, Pam challenges us to do just that. Encouragement is not for just a few, but for all of us. As you read this book, may you be challenged to be an "encourager." When we are in the valley battling cancer or any other adversity, it is so comforting to know that someone cares. My prayer is that you are the one who cares.

In His Love,

David Dravecky
President, Outreach of Hope
Retired Pitcher, San Diego Padres
and San Francisco Giants

Introduction

On October 18, 1995, I was told I had a large mass in my chest, a lymphoma. After a biopsy, the pathologist determined it was Hodgkin's Disease. I knew very little about Hodgkin's Disease, or cancer for that matter.

I was thirty-six years old, healthy, and fit. In fact, I dedicated most of my adult life to keeping myself and others physically fit. I have a university degree in nutrition and am certified as a health fitness instructor. It was my profession and had been for sixteen years. Now my body was being invaded by disease—and not just any disease, but cancer.

This book tells my personal story, gives practical suggestions of support during each phase of a battle with cancer, and it encourages a fighting spirit. It also is about how my family and friends were gifts of God who helped me heal. There is great healing power in care. Being a caregiver, a source of support, and a friend during adversity is not an easy task. It also requires you to bear a heavy load. Unfortunately, we often feel inadequate to do the job and retreat when we are needed the most. This book offers specific ideas on how you can help a friend or loved one at each stage of the illness.

I've included excerpts from my journal in hope of giving you some idea of what your friend may be feeling at each stage. Every person has different needs and reactions, but I believe this book will enable you to relate on a more personal level. I have used the term friend throughout the book for clarity and ease. Whether they be a brother, sister, father, mother, daughter, grandparent, or cousin, I know they also are your friend.

Count it as a privilege that you have the opportunity to help your friend during one of life's darkest moments. You can inspire and influence with love, hope, understanding, compassion, and a positive persistent attitude. Find the special qualities within yourself and discover the difference it makes in others lives when you share those gifts. Do this and no matter what the outcome, you will be helping your friend, loved one, and yourself.

Remember that all acts of kindness are helpful. But your friend is in for the fight of his or her life against a very formidable enemy. There are many things you can do, as family and friends, to really make a difference. God bless you for sharing the burden!

Let us not love with words or tongue but with actions and in truth.

—1 John 3:18

Chapter 1
You Can Make a Difference

In December 1995, two months after I was diagnosed with cancer, my mother, daughter Riley, and I were at a Christmas party. A woman I'd just met said to me, "You're going to make it. I've just been talking to your mother. She told me about all the caring things people are doing to help you. It will make a difference." As I think back on all that has happened during the past year, I realize she was right. The love and support I received were vital to my healing.

My extended family had no experience with cancer or any kind of life-threatening disease, but what they had was a willingness to get involved. They had to face their fears about cancer, head-on, just as I was doing.

I remember telling someone about how a family member was coming to my home for each and every chemotherapy treatment. She replied, "Well, it sure is nice that they're able to do that." But they weren't really able in the way she meant. They all lived more than 500 miles away. They all had jobs, families, and responsibilities of their own. Taking time off work and the continual traveling was a financial strain on them as well. I call it "facing cancer together."

Today we're reaping the rewards of our efforts. The cancer in my body completely disappeared within four months of its discovery, although treatments lasted more than seven months. It hasn't shown itself since, and I believe it never will. Should cancer decide to challenge me again, however, I've found what I never knew I had: the courage to face mortality and the strength to live each day to its fullest. The bonds within my family have been reconfirmed in love, respect and gratitude for each other.

At the time of my diagnosis, my relationship with my father was strained. It had been that way for years. We talked but there was little or no sharing between us. That changed over the course of my battle. He was with me every step of the way.

I received a letter from him recently, in which he spoke of the changes that have occurred in him. His spirituality and belief in God had been reaffirmed. He also said he had an appreciation for life he had never known. Our relationship is better than it has ever been in my adult life. In fact, my whole family is closer than we've been—ever. Cancer is a life-changing experience!

When my treatments ended, I began to look back on all I'd been through to see what made my experience different. I had learned, through a very dear friend's battle with ovarian cancer, that we often feel helpless when cancer strikes someone we love. I learned, through my own experience, that while it's true that friends and family can't directly fight cancer, there are many things they can do that provide much needed strength to the fighter. In my case, it meant taking over the details of everyday life so I could focus all my remaining energy on getting well; giving me hope and inspiration when I felt I couldn't go on; filling my world with a love so powerful it began a healing process that forever changed me; showing me how to love myself.

I hope this book inspires and guides you on just how to do these things for your friend or loved one who has cancer. But don't be surprised if your friend has a difficult time asking for help, or even resists your efforts. We've all been taught that it's a strength to be independent, to not ask for or accept help. Popular scripture holds that it is more blessed to give than to receive. But if we are to give, there must be someone to receive our gifts. I believe the Bible teaches us that it is a form of generosity to accept generosity.

Taking charge of my illness early gave me a better chance of survival. But of equal importance was the ability to ask for and accept help. Even if your friend doesn't ask, do kind deeds for him. Hold her hands when she's frightened or in pain. Talk to him about the future, and give him hope. With each sharing act you do, your friend will soon learn that by accepting help from others, you can also help others.

Find your way together, and the road will take you on a journey of love, hope, and healing. This is true not only for your friend, but also for everyone who has the courage to get involved. In the words of Doctor Bernie Siegel, "love heals. I do not claim that love cures everything, but it can heal and in the process cures occur also."[1]

A friend does not ask "May I help with your load?" but has already carried it far up the road.[2]

—Mary Dawson Hughes

Chapter 2

When You First Hear the News

Journal Entry, October 25, 1995

I'm beginning [this entry] with the events and feelings that occurred in my life on October 18, 1995—Wednesday, October 18—actually called "Black Wednesday" around our house. I was anxious and nervous about my chest X ray that morning. I didn't sleep well Tuesday night and was both ready to find out more information and dreading it. I got up at 8 a.m. and showered. While in the shower, I decided to feel underneath my arm for any lumps. My family doctor told me on Tuesday that I did not have any lumps under my arm. However, I was tender in a spot under my right arm, the same side as the lump in my neck. As I was feeling, there it was . . . a lump under my arm, too. That's when panic set in. I threw on my robe and walked into the kitchen where Jim and

Riley [just nine months old] were having breakfast. I told Jim of my finding.

He hugged me and said it would be all right. "Just get dressed and let's get to the doctor so we can put this whole thing behind us," he said. At the doctor's office I was told that the X ray showed something in my chest and I was being sent for a CAT Scan.

The strangest thing happened to me as we walked into the hospital to have the test. I looked up at the sky and saw the blue more vividly than ever before, as well as the white of the clouds. It was as if I was looking up into the heavens, not at the sky. The same thing happened when we came out of the hospital, although it was not as strong—probably because I was also upset by what I'd learned. But now, with hindsight, I believe I was being given the opportunity to come home. I believe I was actually being given a choice. My decision would not come until later.

Riley, Jim, and I went into the hospital and met the radiologist. She was on her way out, a mix-up in scheduling, but would be back that afternoon to read my results. She promised to call us before 4 p.m.

As I was lying on the table of the big CAT-Scan machine, the radiologist came in to see me. She had looked at my X ray and said, "There is definitely a mass in your chest." When I asked her what that meant, I already knew the answer. She believed she was looking at lymphoma. I lay there not believing this was happening to me. Tears just poured out as the technician performed the CAT Scan. I remember just lying on that table as she gave instructions, following them and thinking that my life was about to end.

Afterwards, I walked back to the room where Jim and Riley were waiting. I knew the doctor hadn't talked to him before she left. When we got outside, I began telling him what I'd learned. I was crying the whole time. He broke down at the car and we just hugged and cried. We were both in shock.

We drove home and waited for the radiologist to call. When she did, I was told that I had a large mass (about the size of a small grapefruit!) in my mediastinum, the area between the lungs that houses the heart. I had fluid between my right lung and rib cage and my liver was swollen, but there did not appear to be any actual mass in the liver.

My feelings went from shock, to disbelief, to strength and a desire to fight, to not knowing what to do. Jim suggested we begin calling family, because it was important to get a support system going.

I also placed a call to my friend, Sabra. I needed understanding that could only be provided by someone who had stood in my shoes just two years earlier. I felt as if she was the only person who could possibly know how I felt. From her words I realized she understood much more than my feelings. She understood the fight that lay before me, and she began to prepare me for it.

Jim and I stayed up that night until almost 2 a.m. and played cards on the bed, knowing we would not sleep. Although I was afraid and unsure about many things, I felt a comfort that told me the news from now on would be good. That feeling gave me some strength. However, I still had a long way to go.

We didn't sleep well, and I was up before 8 a.m. on Thursday, October 19. My friend Diane had called the night before to say she was returning home to Denver in case I needed her. Another friend, Karen, called that morning and said, "I'm coming too." I initially protested, saying there was nothing she could do to help. Although I didn't know what I needed, somehow she did. She replied, "If you would rather me stay at John and Diane's house, I will do that, but I want to be close just in case you need me." Great friends!

My friend Katie came and picked up Riley so Jim and I could go to see our family doctor and have some time together to digest all of this. We asked for our doctor's assistance in getting in to see a surgeon. I knew it was a lymphoma, but there are twelve different kinds, and I wanted a biopsy as soon as possible. The not knowing and waiting, the state of limbo, was very difficult for me and, I believe, even harder for Jim. The soonest we could get the procedure done was Monday and the results of the biopsy would take five to seven days. That felt like an eternity.

We went to Jim's restaurant to update his management team on my condition. They have all been so helpful to us. I felt sad but strong talking to them. That is also how I felt when I talked to my family.

Jim, on the other hand, has broken down each time. I am sad for him. The best thing that came out of the meeting, though, was a contact to the University Hospital Cancer Center in Denver. Jim and I went home and had a few hours together and by ourselves. I was still seeing the "death demons" and fighting images of life without me. The biggest image is the thought that my daughter won't even remember me! It scared me at the time, but now I believe it was all a process I had to go through to reach a decision.

Karen and Diane flew into Denver, picked up Riley from Katie's house and came with lots of food and support. John [Diane's husband] also came down after work to join us. I excused myself early while everyone continued to visit. The company was great for Jim, but I knew I needed to be alone to work on my thoughts. I remember talking to the cancer in my bedroom, saying, "I am not the victim, you are." That thought became more and more powerful to me. I meditated for the first "real" time in my life. I cleared my mind—really stopped the thoughts and voices—and everything was still. I could listen to my body and, ultimately, to God.

I came away from that experience strong and confident that I would prevail. I have meditated every night since. That was a big turning point for me physically and mentally. I had been given a choice, and I choose life.

When you learn that a friend or loved one has cancer, your first reaction may be shock. In addition, you may feel helpless. But helplessness doesn't have to overcome you. There are so many things you can do to let your friend know she's not alone. Don't be afraid to talk about cancer. Don't wait for your friend to ask for help. Get involved from the very beginning and let your friend know that you're there for the duration. I was so afraid of what my future held, and the friends and family who came to my side immediately let me know that they, too, were willing to carry a load. From every card I received and every phone call that was made, I gained strength within.

Here are some ideas on how you can lift the load for your friend when a diagnosis of cancer has just been made.

Be There

If you're a family member or close friend, just being there is comforting. However, it's important not to overwhelm your friend with your presence or the presence of too many others. Your friend's privacy is also important at times. Be open to your friend's need for privacy. (Hopefully, she will let you know when she wants your company.) Organizing one or two persons to help with food, childcare, handling telephone calls, or just sitting and waiting in support is great.

Your friend may not even realize how alone he or she feels right now. My mother wanted to come immediately but needed her own time to process the news. Karen, my best friend from childhood, filled that role.

It is very important that whoever comes is emotionally stable, at least outwardly. The last thing your friend needs right now is to be providing emotional comfort to someone else.

A small group of supportive family and friends may be best. Talk among yourselves and decide who is best able to provide support. Your friend will need all of you throughout the next months.

Your friend may feel there's no reason for anyone to come. I felt that way initially. I didn't know how to accept support. I had no idea what I needed. Visiting is a judgment call you'll have to make. But I drew my strength from the love that surrounded me, and I'm thankful my friends were there.

Telephone Calls

A word of caution—telephone calls can be overwhelming. I became exhausted from *talking* about what was happening, on top of being exhausted from what was *actually* happening.

Unless you're a very close friend, wait a few days or even weeks before you call. Better yet, call a family member (not in the same household) who can give you an insight into the situation, someone who can explain the diagnosis to you and save your friend from having to do it.

Also, this person can let you know if your friend wants and needs phone calls. If you're a close friend or family member, you might take on this role yourself. You can become the information link for others. I had two friends who did this and it relieved me of numerous phone calls I wasn't ready to handle. They kept a list of who had called, and they passed it on to me so that I knew who had checked on me. These friends also made phone calls to other friends, encouraging prayers and support.

Your friend will want to hear from you, but please be sensitive to the fact that he or she is facing a life-threatening illness, an overload of information, and many pressing decisions to make.

Childcare

If your friend has children, childcare is a major concern. There are numerous trips to doctors' offices. There also is a need for time to be alone or with a spouse. You can volunteer to take the kids or watch them at their house. Don't wait to be asked, just make the offer.

Bring or Send Food

For a family with children, bringing or sending food can be very helpful. Believe me, no one in your friend's household feels like cooking. The role that food plays in the prevention and treatment of cancer is very well documented, so you want to be sure your friend can eat what you prepare. It's always important to find out about any dietary restrictions. The convenience of visits to drop off food is important too. If you want to bring food, call ahead to schedule a time.

Bringing food that requires little clean-up, or preparing a meal at your friend's home and cleaning up afterwards, is another thoughtful gesture. You can, for example, bring food in disposable containers. This eliminates the need for keeping up with dishes and getting them returned to their proper owners. Our friends brought food to our house, cooked there, and cleaned up afterwards. We were in the waiting stage, so this was a great way to support us and help at the same time.

Send Money

Even if your friend has health insurance, the financial costs of treating cancer are tremendous. Many therapies are not covered by insurance, and those that are covered usually require the insured to pay a percentage of the cost. Even with all the financial help we received from family and friends, it will be years before we pay off the accumulated debt.

Your friend may not be comfortable talking about this, but believe me, any money you can send will be greatly appreciated. If you're uncomfortable with this idea, designate the money be used for something specific. Several ways you can do this are included in the following chapters. No amount of money is too small or too great. Just send an amount that is meaningful and comfortable to you. You may chose to send one financial gift, or several. Your friend needs to focus on getting well and, far too often, the financial worries get in the way. Your financial support will ease this burden.

Send a Card

Sending a card or cards takes so little effort and is a thoughtful way to show your concern. Don't just let the card do your talking, though. Take some time to include some heartfelt words.

I remember receiving a letter from a college friend I hadn't spoken to in years. She shared with me some of the challenges she had faced in her adult life and encouraged me in my struggle. I was so touched by her willingness to reach out to me.

Cards can be sent throughout the ordeal to remind your friend of your constant thoughts and prayers. Your friend needs to know these things and will appreciate them.

Send a Book

Your friend is preparing to battle a very formidable enemy and must be armed with as much information as possible. There are so many books available on the subject of cancer that it can be difficult to know where to begin. Select a book you would like to have if you found yourself in the same condition. Evaluate what stage your friend is in with his or her battle with cancer and choose books accordingly. At the initial diagnosis, for example, books on treatment options, as well as books that explain cancer in more detail, will be helpful.

Send books that tell the story of someone who beat the odds and is living healthy today. No matter how grave the situation, there is always testimonial of someone who overcame it. These kinds of books are extremely important in developing that fighter spirit. (In "For Further Reading," I've listed books I found helpful, along with a brief description of each.)

Every book I received was an opportunity for me to learn, grow, and take charge of my illness. There are many people who have struggled with cancer and survived. Providing your friend with their stories, wisdom, and insights can be a powerful weapon in his or her battle. If you can't make a decision on a book, send a gift certificate from a bookstore.

Get on the Internet

There's a lot of information about cancer on the Internet. Get on the computer and find information for your friend. My brother did this for me. I gave him topics I was interested in and he did the searching. It saved me a lot of time, quickly providing me with the information I needed. There are also personal stories on the Internet that your friend will be able to relate to. One woman had kept a journal of her battle with Hodgkin's Disease, the same cancer I was diagnosed with, and had put it on a web page. I found the information very insightful and easily accessible.

Learn about Cancer Yourself

Learning about your friend's illness is a simple, yet significant, way to show you care. Information about cancer is available from a number of sources, including the National Cancer Institute. You can call the institute at 1-800-4-CANCER to request information. Consider buying a book on cancer, going to the library or getting on the Internet. The American Cancer Society, for example, has a Web site: <http:www.cancer.org>.Take the time to learn what living with cancer is like.

Accompany Them on Doctor Visits

Your friend is receiving more information than can be processed by one person. Yet, the information is crucial, because it will be the basis for deciding on a treatment plan. Your friend will need help gathering and recording all the information, especially if your friend doesn't have a spouse or close companion to help. But even if there is someone, it's a good idea to have an extra pair of ears.

After receiving my diagnosis, for example, my husband and I brought a notebook and a small tape recorder to every doctor visit. We were both out of sorts, and it took all our concentration to focus on the words being told to us. It was very helpful to have a friend there to take notes and operate the recorder. My friends also had questions I hadn't thought of asking. When friends cared enough to be with me at the many doctor visits I had to make, I experienced great support.

Begin a Prayer Chain / Encourage Others

Ask everyone you know for their love, support, and prayers for your friend. You may speak to people in person, call, write, or use the Internet to organize people. If they ask what they can do to help, encourage them to send cards and say prayers.

Knowing that people all over the world were praying for me was empowering. Call churches or religious organizations and ask that your friend be included in their prayer time. Pray with your friend. Offer a healing ceremony or ritual if your friend is open to it.

THINGS *NOT* TO DO:

1. *Don't send flowers.* While flowers are nice, your friend will be receiving enough of them and there are more useful ways to spend your money. I appreciated flowers more when they came later, as a celebration.

2. *Don't leave phone messages asking your friend to return your calls.* Your friend is overwhelmed, so please recognize that returning phone calls is not a priority at this time and only adds to the stress. Do call and leave messages expressing your love and concern. Also state that you will call back at a later time.

3. *Don't visit your friend in large groups.* Send a designated friend or a couple of designated friends to convey everyone's care and support. Do this only if your friend wants visitors.

4. *Don't become overly emotional in front of your friend.* Crying with your friend is certainly appropriate, but don't put your friend in the position of comforter. It is time for you to be supportive and strong. Look to others to provide you with the support you'll need during this time.

5. *Don't sit back and do nothing.* This is a time when you're greatly needed. Get involved by offering your time, money, or services in any way you can. Encourage others to do the same. Don't abandon your friend when you're needed the most.

Therefore encourage one another
and build each other up,
just as in fact you are doing.

—1 Thessalonians 5:11

Chapter 3
What To Say and What Not to Say

Many people don't know what to say to a friend who has just been diagnosed with cancer. I know because that's how I felt when one of my dear friends was stricken with the disease. I also know this awkwardness is true by the long silences on the other end of the phone during calls from my friends.

What do you say that is helpful and what do you not say that may be hurtful? I've put together a list of both to guide you in talking to your friend. All these comments were made to me either verbally or in writing. I realize every word was meant to show love and support for me but without sufficient thought and understanding, these words can often do more harm than good. I hope this will give you a better understanding of what and what not to say and why. Use your own judgment when determining what is appropriate for your friend and when to say it. Speak from your heart.

What to Say:

1. *I'm so sorry this is happening to you.* Empathy and understanding are needed now. Your friend is also sorry it's happening. Hearing these words can bring a sense of unity between the two of you.

2. *You're one of the strongest people I know. If anyone can beat cancer, you can.* If you truly feel this way, say it—if not, don't. I found these words empowering when spoken with truth and sincerity.

3. *My thoughts and prayers are with you every day.* There is nothing your friend needs more than prayers. Remember, you don't want these to be empty words, so pray every day.

4. *May God continue to bless you with his healing.* As healing begins to take place, whether emotionally, physically, or spiritually, these words are comforting to hear.

5. *I'm here for you.* This is a nice reminder and a relief to hear, provided it's the truth.

6. *You're an inspiration to me.* As your friend faces these challenges with courage and strength, tell him or her how inspiring it is to others. It helped me to see some purpose to my suffering.

7. *We're saying prayers of love and healing for you, and I know these prayers are heard.* Faith is all we have to carry us through many challenges in our lives. This is certainly true with cancer. Knowing that friends were praying and that they believed in prayer helped me believe, too.

8. *Keep remembering that each new day brings you one step closer to the end of this whole ordeal.* This comment helped a lot when I was beginning to doubt whether I could go on. Many cancer patients stop treatments before they're complete due to the intensity and severity of side effects. Encouraging your friend to face each day with hope, one at a time, can give him or her the strength to make it through.

9. *We're praying for a complete and full recovery.* Specific prayers are better than general prayers; they add personalization and offer hope.

10. *I want you to know that I will walk beside you and I will always be there for you.* Cancer

is terrifying. Knowing they won't be alone can lessen cancer patients' fears. This is what your friend needs to hear.

11. *May God bless you and give you strength for your challenge.* I found this statement to show empathy and understanding because I, too, knew I needed the strength that only God could provide.

12. *Remember there are a lot of people who care for you and are willing to do whatever they can to help you.* Cancer is a rough road and it's comforting to know that many people care along the way. This is a good reminder to your friend that people really do want to help and that he or she can let them.

13. *So many people love you. Think of yourself encircled in a shield of love and prayers.* Not only is this an expression of love and support, it's also a beautiful thought for meditation and visualization.

14. *I've put you on a prayer list, and more and more people are praying for you every day.* Tell your friend about the prayer list and how many people are involved. I was so thankful to hear about each and every prayer being said for me.

15. *Your courageous attitude is a blessing to your family and an example to others.* I found this compliment very powerful. It gave me hope that my suffering was not in vain.

16. *May God be with you and fill you with his strength, comfort, and love.* Only God can provide the resources needed to get through this battle.

17. *I know you must feel terrible. Please talk to me about it anytime because I really care.* Give your friend an open door to talk to you. This also lets your friend know you understand he or she is in pain.

What *Not* to Say:

1. *I know how difficult this is for you and your family.* Do you really? If you have not been through cancer yourself, don't believe you can begin to know how difficult it is.

2. *I understand how you must be feeling.* Have you ever had to fight for your life, felt pain and sickness every day, had your hair fall out? If not, you don't understand. Your friend doesn't expect you to understand; rather, your friend is just hoping you'll be there.

3. *Please let me know if there's anything I can do to help.* There are so many things you can do. Take initiative, and just do them.

4. *What are your chances for survival?* This is not a helpful or encouraging question. If your friend wants to share this information, fine, but don't ask. For every predicted survival rate, there has been someone who beat the odds. This is what you want your friend to focus on.

5. *This must be God's will for you.* This statement is of no comfort and can hurt your friend deeply.

6. *There must be some sin in your life for which God is disciplining you.* You don't know this, and if you believe that God works in this way, by all means keep it to yourself. Your friend does not need additional guilt and confusion from you.

7. *Of all people to get cancer, you're the last one I would have ever thought would get it.* This comment can make your friend feel alienated, as if he or she is somehow very different. Cancer has many causes and is not necessarily selective.

8. *You were so active and healthy. It just goes to show you that it doesn't matter how you live your life.* This reflects an insensitivity to your friend's dignity. It does matter how we live our lives, and your friend understands that better than most people will ever know.

9. *Things could be worse. . . .* Certainly they could, but they're bad enough right now.

10. *Look on the bright side. . . .* It's very difficult for your friend to see any "bright side."

11. *You have the same cancer as my friend in college; . . . he died.* Please don't share stories that don't have happy endings. Your friend has enough fear to deal with, so don't add to it.

Friendship is one of the sweetest joys of life. Many might have failed beneath the bitterness of their trial had they not found a friend.[3]

—Charles Haddon Spurgeon

Chapter 4
When Treatment Is Decided

Journal Entry, October 20, 1995

Got a call from an oncologist, the contact we had made through Jim's business. A doctor calling me asking what he can do to help? I like him already. He said he would get me into surgery today, so Jim and I rushed to Denver to the Cancer Center. Thank goodness Karen was here to keep Riley. I went into surgery with two residents and the surgeon. After about forty-five minutes, the one-inch piece of my lymph node was out and on its way to the pathologist. Jim, Diane, John, and I then sat through a meeting with one of the oncologists. She gave me the first diagnosis of Hodgkin's Disease. I was ecstatic to hear this because Hodgkin's Disease is one of the most treatable of all lymphomas. A week ago I would have been devastated to hear I had Hodgkin's but, under the circumstances, Hodgkin's was the best news I could have received. We all felt very positive after that meeting. We came back to the house, and Diane cooked dinner for us again.

October 23, 1995

We had an appointment with my oncologist today. I had lots of support as Jim, Karen, Diane, and my mother were all with me. We hoped to receive the official results from the biopsy. I also had to have a bone marrow biopsy. None of this is fun! The initial response from the pathologist was still Hodgkin's but now we were determining what type of Hodgkin's. I am classified as a Stage II A, which means above the diaphragm and no symptoms; although, treatments will be for a Stage IV due to the size of the tumor. I like my doctor—great wisdom, very humble, not a "know it all."

October 30, 1995

Tomorrow I start chemotherapy at 9 a.m. I'm a little anxious, shaky, unsure of the whole thing. There are so many books, tapes, and people who warn you against chemotherapy that I'm confused. But the survival rates with this treatment are good and I believe I need to use all resources to fight. I just wish I knew what caused it so I could fix it.

I lost it today on the way to the Cancer Center. I was feeling stressed, feeling too much pressure. I wanted Jim to take that away from me, but he can't. Sabra told me that she just thought of it as a "bad flu" that she had to take medicine for but would soon be gone. Maybe that is the best way. . . . I will have to find the best approach for me. I'm on information overload as it is right now, so I'll give myself time and space to develop.

Determining a treatment plan is a difficult decision to make. The best thing you can do at this point is to make sure your friend has everything needed to make an informed decision. Then, be ready to support that decision wholeheartedly. The decision is a very personal matter and you should keep your opinion to yourself unless it's specifically asked for.

Again, support is the key word now. The battle with cancer is as much mental as it is physical. Your friend is in charge of this war, and you want to encourage that fighting spirit by remaining loyal to the battle plan—even if you don't agree with it. If your friend is lacking that spirit, continue feeling it and acting on it yourself. It might be contagious. Don't give your friend any reason to doubt his or her ability to be cured.

No matter what the prognosis, doubt can, and probably will, plague your friend from time to time. If he or she needs to express those doubts, listen. Continue to encourage hope and healing.

The following sections are the things I found to be most helpful at this time:

Organize a Support Team

A support team is needed throughout the next several months, possibly years. It's imperative that your friend never feels alone in the fight with cancer. No doubt, there will be days when extra effort is needed, such as for surgery, hospital stays, chemotherapy, or radiation treatment. Sometimes support will be needed the whole week, depending upon your friend's response to the illness and treatment. It takes a team of friends and family responding together according to some plan to provide this kind of continuous support.

My younger sister took on this time-consuming task even though she lived in another state, had two small children at home, and worked a full time job. But what my family and close friends provided to Jim, Riley, and me in the way of support can never be measured. Someone was at my home for every chemotherapy session I endured. They took care of Riley so Jim could sit with me for the four to six hours required to pump the drugs into my body. They stayed for the days that followed when I was too fatigued and nauseated to even get out of bed. They enabled Jim to be at his restaurant, opened less than one year, so business did not suffer.

Most of all, they gave Riley the love and emotional availability she needed at a time I wasn't always able to. They gave Jim the reprieve he needed from having so many responsibilities. They gave me the time and energy to focus on healing.

This wasn't easy for anyone who came to stay and care for us. It meant plane trips or long drives. But it was critical to my recovery, and I can never fully express my gratitude.

One of my team members called to check on me following every blood test and doctor visit I made. This person then let me know they would be calling others who were waiting for the news. They had educated themselves so they understood test results and areas of concern, including all possible side effects from the eight different chemotherapy drugs I was taking. It seemed everything I felt that I might need was provided without my asking.

I asked my sister how they knew what to do. She said, "We just listened. We listened to what you said, what you were able to do, and how you sounded. Then we all talked among ourselves to determine how we could support you." Then they contacted close friends who had asked when and how they could help in the plan. If I had to pick one thing that meant the most to me, it would be this empathy and attunement.

Organize a Fund-Raiser

Whether it be dinners, auctions, sports tournaments, or raffle drawings, all that is needed is someone to organize. You'll find there are lots of individuals, groups, and businesses that will support you, especially when they learn that the cause is for a friend. Jim's business partners sold raffle tickets for prize money at their company Christmas party. Generosity poured out of the employees, vendors, and business associates who participated. Even those who won prize money donated it to us.

There are many people who want to help, but don't know what to do. Fund-raisers are a great way to get everyone involved. It just takes a leader.

Track Down a Survivor

Find the name and address of a survivor of your friend's type of cancer, preferably one who has chosen the same treatment plan. Your friend will probably be given the name of someone by his or her doctor, but if not, ask for your friend. Then make the contact and attempt to arrange a meeting or phone call between your friend and the survivor. This person can provide your friend with first-hand knowledge of how to survive cancer.

Send Newspaper Articles or Books

Any materials you can find on cancer survivors is great. Continue to provide your friend with the mental picture that he or she can survive too. Libraries and bookstores are good places to look for news articles, magazines, and books. Don't collect materials about cancer deaths or survival rates.

Create a Call Chain

It's too stressful and often expensive for the one battling cancer to also constantly update folks on new information or test results. I remember one of my friends being upset that Jim or I hadn't called to tell her I was in the hospital. Under normal circumstances, that would be understandable, but these are not normal times—hospital stays can be frequent. Again, your friend is overwhelmed and fighting for life.

Take it upon yourself to call your friend or a family member on a weekly basis to get updates. Write down days of tests or doctor visits so you can stay informed. Better yet, start a call chain to keep everyone you know updated. Your effort will relieve your friend of this time-consuming task.

Send Phone Cards

Prepaid long distance cards are a great way to show you really mean it when you say, "Call me if you ever need to talk." It's also financially helpful as long distance bills can soar during this time. Mine doubled—at least. Usually there are out-of-town friends or family and, as in my case, the doctor may be in another city or even state. Sending these phone cards can make things much easier for your friend.

Give Gift Certificates to Health Food Stores

According to the American Cancer Society Cancer Statistics, diet is the leading cause of cancer mortality in the United States (just ahead of tobacco). I learned this fact from a book my mother gave me.

I made necessary changes in my eating habits. Knowing I was doing this, a friend had the idea of giving gift certificates to a health food market. It was a great way to show support and, at the time, more helpful than flowers. Gift certificates can also replace the discomfort some people feel about sending money.

Buying organic produce and supplements becomes very costly. Gift certificates not only reduce those costs for your friend, but they also give them many options. In addition to food and supplements, most health food stores carry juicers and a wide variety of books.

Contact your local health-food store or co-op. They can assist you in setting up a gift certificate program. Most purchases can be made over the phone, so it's easy for everyone involved. If your friend is going this route, it's a big help.

Prepare a Travel Bag

A friend prepared a travel bag for me, and it was such a great idea. She filled a gym bag with magazines, cards, travel games, food, bottled water, and napkins for the long doctor visits and treatment sessions we were about to endure. It also included a pillow and blanket so I could sleep on the drive home, and sealable plastic bags for possible vomiting. Be creative with your travel bag, imagining what your friend might need. My friend thought of more possibilities than I could have at the time. When the treatments were over, I returned everything to her with much gratitude in my heart.

Help With Hotel Costs

Sometimes treatments take place in another city. In my case, it was in Denver, which is about seventy-five miles from home. Luckily, I was able to take my treatments as an outpatient. But I know of people who must stay in the hospital days at a time to receive treatments.

Every cancer case and treatment is different. If your friend is in the hospital, a hotel for the spouse or family is a thoughtful gift. My neighbor's company made arrangements for her to have a hotel room while her husband was in the hospital for tests and chemotherapy (a great way a business can help using their corporate discount). Keep in mind that if your friend's doctor is in another city, extended stays there might be frequent, and costs add up quickly.

Miscellaneous Items Needed

There are many miscellaneous items that can help a friend who is undergoing treatment for cancer. For example, taking a shower can be extremely difficult for a person receiving chemotherapy, radiation, or who is recovering from surgery. A shower stool can be a thoughtful gift to help your friend with this task.

There are other gifts that can help your friend through the little daily tasks that are often taken for granted. While on chemotherapy drugs, for example, shaving with a razor is discouraged due to the possibility of open wounds (nicks and cuts make it easier for infection to set in when the body's immune system is compromised). A gift of an an electric shaver is as thoughtful as it is useful. Your friend will need sleep to heal, so a mask to place over the eyes and earplugs can make the sleep more restful. Earplugs are especially needed if your friend spends any time in the hospital. Hospitals can be very loud places—even at 3 a.m.!

Things *Not* to Do:

1. *Don't express a lack of confidence in the treatment plan.* Clearly, your friend needs words of confidence and assurance. If you do

doubt the treatment, keep this doubt to yourself.

2. *Don't suggest another doctor or cancer center unless there is a real reason to believe one is needed.* Don't base a need for change solely on your feelings and opinions.

3. *Don't make casual visits.* This is a time for carrying a load. If you live out of town and go to see your friend, plan to work, and make that clear from the start. Your friend doesn't need to be preparing meals, washing sheets, and cleaning the house for guests right now. Unless you are sure your friend wants you there, save your visits for another time.

Christ has no body on earth but yours, yours are the only hands with which He can do His work, yours are the only feet with which He can go about the world, yours are the only eyes through which His compassion can shine forth upon a troubled world. Christ has no body on earth now but yours.[4]

—St. Teresa of Avila

Chapter 5
During Treatment: Encouraging Acts

Journal Entry December 11, 1995

Tomorrow is chemotherapy day—again! It seems like they come too soon, and I am finding myself more anxious about them. Today I cried on Jim's shoulder just at the thought of it. I think it's because I know that I won't feel well for several days, and because I'm beginning to really feel the difference in a chemo week and non-chemo week. Also, I had a tough time coming out of the last "double dose" of chemotherapy and surgery performed on the same day [to put in my catheter].

We set up the Christmas tree last night. It was both a fiasco and great fun! Riley was so tired from running errands with me all afternoon, she fell asleep before the tree was decorated. But this morning she was wide-eyed looking at it. This evening when we came in, it was dark except for the lights on the tree. She looked at it with wonder and appreciation and just said, "Ohhh!" That is how I want to be again. . . .

Mother drove in tonight. She will be so helpful to me. I really need to do some visualization to prepare for tomorrow. Visualizing my body destroying the cancer gives me strength. Visualizing Jim and me in our old age together, and being here as Riley grows up, brings me peace. I need to find both strength and peace tonight to alleviate the anxiety building inside me.

December 12, 1995

No chemotherapy today. My white blood cells were too low—a total of 1700 and only 300 neutrophil. They won't administer chemotherapy to anyone with less than a 1500 neutrophil count. I wasn't even close! So it's self-administered shots everyday, stay away from people who are sick, large crowds, or small children in day care. Chemotherapy is postponed for a week.

We stopped by the whole foods market after the cancer center. I talked with the nutritionist there who was alarmed at my neutrophil count. This is an everyday occurrence for the cancer patient, though.

She also shared with me that, in her experience, most cancer patients seemed to have deep-rooted anger they were not aware of. That has been on my mind and I think deserves some exploration. I'm also going to explore the stressful events that happened in my life one to three years prior to diagnosis. I may even need to go back further . . .

February 8, 1996

It's been longer than one month since I have written. A lot has transpired . . . My friend DeDe came to help out for ten days. My older sister, Paula, came for eight days. It was good to have her here, very comforting for me. She's great with Riley. Dad is here now.

I've been struggling with the fear that I won't beat this cancer, or if I do . . . how long before it comes back. I just got down on my knees and prayed to God for some relief from this fear. It's amazing I feel such comfort. I just want to live so badly, and I now know everything will be all right.

I believe God was telling me that I'll be here on Earth for many more years. And if not, that will be okay, too. (But I sure hope I'll be here!) I guess this is where my faith really comes in. I'm feeling pretty nauseated this time. I'm having lots of fatigue, nausea, and depression. This is no fun!

March 15, 1996

Well, recovery from the treatments are getting longer and harder. I'm still getting lots of help from family—what would I do without them? I seem to be feeling alienated, as if no one can understand where I am and what I'm going through . . .

Since there is "no evidence of disease" anymore, I'm going to get my doctor's opinion about skipping the radiation treatments. I don't know how much more of this I can take!

Things can get really rough for your friend, especially if he or she has opted for one of the "big three": chemotherapy, radiation, or surgery. Often times, it's not just one, but two, or even all three of the treatments. They each can take a devastating toll on the body.

Alternative treatments, which include nutrition, acupuncture, and others, can play a supportive role in helping the body combat the effects of the "big three" by decreasing pain, minimizing damage to healthy cells, and promoting recovery. Encourage your friend as my oncologist encouraged me when I asked what treatments I should use along with the prescribed chemotherapy and radiation. He said, "Whatever works for you, do it."

Many fellow cancer warriors have told me about all of the friends and family they heard from in the beginning. But when it came time for treatment, or later as treatments became almost unbearable, their support system was no longer there. Please, don't let this happen to your friend. Maintain contact and encourage him or her to remain strong. This is when you're needed most. Hang in there, because it can get extremely difficult, not only for your friend, but for everyone involved. Remember, you are making a difference.

Be There

Just being with your friend means so much. This is where organizing a support team can really help out. Whether you live in or out of town, you can usually arrange your schedule to be there at some point during treatment. Depending on the type of cancer, surgery often is the first step in determining what treatment will be recommended. It is important that close friends and/or family be at the hospital during surgery to provide needed support to the immediate family, especially should news be less than encouraging.

Being there to help out during chemotherapy or radiation treatments can give your friend the energy to concentrate on healing. Those close to the cancer patient can be of greater assistance if they know what to look for. Educate yourself on the needs of your friend. What are the possible complications after surgery? What are the side effects of the chemotherapy drugs? What should be done in the event of a fever or allergic reaction? If you're staying with your friend during treatment, it's necessary to know the answers to these and other questions.

Help with Health Care Claims

One of the young men in our cancer group was having extreme difficulty with his insurance company. He was making no progress understanding the claims (what was approved, what wasn't, and why). He was very sick and had no energy to deal with this situation, and he did not have a spouse or family to help him.

One night at our group meeting, a woman new to the group, told us that she filed health care claims for a living, and she offered to volunteer her services if anyone needed help. She was another answered prayer. We quickly put her in touch with the young man.

Managing insurance matters can be a very difficult task. Fortunately, my husband took care of the insurance himself, leaving me free from the stress of it all. But I know he could have used help at times, too. If insurance is your area of knowledge or expertise, your friend will appreciate your services.

Housecleaning and Lawn Care

Housecleaning and lawn care quickly go by the wayside during a battle with cancer. Although it's important to maintain order and harmony in the home, frankly, there's little time or energy to focus on accomplishing these tasks. Hiring a cleaning service or lawn service can be a great relief during this time.

Knowing the financial toll cancer was taking on us, a very dear friend gathered up donations from other friends and hired a cleaning service for our home for a period of three months. Hearing about it, other friends and family pitched in, buying two weeks, one month, whatever they could afford.

Before I knew it, we had a cleaning service for the duration of my chemotherapy treatments and a during a few months of my recovery as well. I was so thankful every time someone came to clean my home. Not only did it remind me of the generosity of my friends and family, it also meant I would have a clean and orderly home. Since I was seldom able to go out, this was very comforting to me.

Bring Food

As mentioned earlier, gifts of food are welcome, especially now when your friend may be going through or recovering from surgery. Remember to call for dietary restrictions and to bring food in disposable containers.

Child Care

Concern for the emotional and physical welfare of the children is a large issue for the parent fighting cancer. Your friend needs peace of mind and focus going into the treatments. In addition to treatments, there are continual tests, blood work, and the almost inevitable hospital stay. Knowing that the children are being taken care of gives your friend one less thing to worry about.

Find out your friend's schedules and volunteer to take the children. A friend of mine, who had a daughter close to Riley's age, invited Riley to her home every Tuesday and Thursday for the day. It was a standing offer. All I did was call and let her know if someone would be bringing Riley. Because I had help from my family during treatments, I frequently dropped Riley off during tests or when I needed rest. It was healthy for Riley, too, as she loved playing with her friend.

Call ahead and invite the kids out for a day with your family or just over to your house for a visit.

Car Pool

If your friend has children who are involved in activities, such as sports, music lessons, or school, volunteer to drive their children to the necessary destinations. Driving while undergoing treatment may be too stressful and difficult for your friend.

Your friend's children might be in a car pool. You can offer to take your friend's turns driving. You might even start a car pool if none exists and offer to drive for your friend.

Run Errands

If you live near your friend, consider running errands for him or her. These daily tasks can become too much for the person undergoing chemotherapy or radiation. Extra responsibilities during holidays also may be quite overwhelming. You can, for example, offer to wrap gifts, mail packages, and run needed errands.

Go Wig Shopping

Your friend will know what the chances are for hair loss based on the protocol for treating her particular cancer. If the odds are high, your friend may choose to wear a wig. Although patients are warned of potential hair loss, when it actually starts to happen, it becomes another devastating blow. That's why it's important to be prepared.

Take your friend wig shopping before her hair falls out. Make it a fun day for her (I don't mean to exclude the men, but I can't imagine a group of men bonding over toupees!) My friend, Diane, and my younger sister, Tricia, took me wig shopping in Denver. To show their support, several other friends had pitched in some money and a card. We went to lunch and then spent the afternoon giggling over all of the possibilities I had for a new look. It was great fun and turned a depressing time into a very happy memory.

Drive Them to Treatment

I was surprised to find that many of the patients in the chemotherapy room were there alone, having driven themselves to the Cancer Center. This is something your friend probably won't ask you to do. You need to ask. Simply inquire, "Who's taking you in for treatment?" If the answer is "nobody," please volunteer to drive. If at all possible, stay during the treatment as well. If you're not comfortable with this, find someone who is. The apprehension of this day and the ones that follow will be lessened when shared with a friend.

Music and Meditation Tapes

If you're a music fan, purchase a tape of special songs for your friend. Sabra told me her favorite gift of support was a cassette tape given to her by a friend.

If your friend is practicing visualization, relaxation, or meditation, there are many excellent tapes available for purchase. You can even find ones that focus on cancer.

As treatments became exceedingly difficult to handle, I found that these tapes helped guide me through them. When the tapes come from a friend, it's a lasting reminder that someone cares.

Send Books

Send books that focus on getting your friend through treatment. Due to the extreme toll it takes on the body, it's not unusual for a cancer patient to stop treatment before it's complete. Books of encouragement and understanding are needed. Look to "For Further Reading" as a guide to help you in your selection.

Send Scriptures, Prayers, and Meditations

As I mentioned, encouragement and understanding are needed now. That is why I so appreciated the scriptures, prayers, and meditations I received. It takes very little effort to write one of these down on a sheet of paper and slip it into a card. These, along with prayer, are what got me through some of the darkest days of my life. My favorite ones are listed in the back of this book.

Decorate the Hospital Room

Being in the hospital is depressing enough, but being in the cancer wing is unbelievable and terrifying. Any kind of decoration is a connection to the outside world. Some suggestions are posters of scriptures, prayers, and meditations; fresh cut flowers or wildflowers; or holiday decorations, if appropriate, such as Christmas trees, the American flag, etc. Food baskets are also a good idea when filled with healthy, nutritious foods.

Be a Patient Advocate

As I mentioned, the cancer ward is a depressing place to find yourself. Also, if your friend is in the hospital, chances are he or she is at one of their weakest moments physically, emotionally, and mentally. A friend who has experience with hospitals, cancer, and/or medicine can be a big help right now.

If you don't have experience but have an assertive personality, you'll do just fine. I found myself so fatigued that I couldn't even stay up with all of the tests, blood work, poking and prodding that was being done to me. Having someone there to speak and act on behalf of the patient is really important. If you fit the description, this job is for you.

Donate Vacation Time

This is where coworkers can help. Paid time off can often be used up during diagnosis and treatment. Because of the costs incurred in addition to normal living expenses, it's imperative that a paycheck continue to come in. Unfortunately, if your friend doesn't have insurance for short- or long-term disability, the paycheck will stop when vacation and sick days are used up. I've heard of some companies that allow employees to donate vacation time to coworkers with cancer. What a great idea!

Another useful thought is to ask coworkers to donate one day's pay, or even two or three—whatever they can afford to offer. Often your company can do this through payroll deductions. If these are not options, talk with management to find creative ways to help your friend in the workplace. But most of all, be encouraging, understanding, and patient.

Things *Not* to Do:

1. *Don't abandon the warrior.* Don't be a "fair-weather friend."

2. *Don't tempt your friend to deviate from the treatment plan in any way.* If you're staying in his or her home, help with medication, supplements, and nutrition. Your friend's mind may not be as alert as when he or she is healthy. Keep alcohol and foods that can increase side effects out of the home.

3. *Don't expose your friend to sickness or infectious diseases to which you have been exposed.* Think about this before any contact with your friend or your friend's family.

It is one of the most beautiful compensations of this life that no man can sincerely try to help another without also helping himself.[5]

—Ralph Waldo Emerson

Chapter 6
Supporting the Recovery Process

Journal Entry August 24, 1996

I feel I'm getting stronger physically. It has been three months since my last and final chemotherapy treatment, and I'm slowly but surely getting some strength back.

I now realize that my inability to sleep was associated with the upcoming visit to my oncologist. Those visits scared me more than I realized or cared to admit at the time. But that's certainly understandable. I'm happy to be aware of it now so I can begin to love and support myself through it. It is a part of my life now.

August 26, 1996

What an extraordinary experience I had last night on my journey toward health and healing. During my meditation, I went to sources of discomfort in my body. One area was my stomach and colon. In it I found a big ball of knots. They'd been there for some time, as they were tan colored but rusted.

I began to ask my body what the source of the knots was. The answers appeared as a white light. One was trying to please other people. I feel myself tighten up in the same place in my body just upon writing that. Also, I was not taking care of myself; I was not recognizing feelings or acknowledging them. I choose not to do that any more. I was blaming myself and letting my critic control my life. Just writing about it releases it again and helps me relax.

My colon is no longer knotted. I've released the knots, untied them, let the emotions flow through my body.

I went into my chest where I saw guilt as a big, black blob, swelling my lymph nodes into cancer. It was no longer there as the lymph nodes, although still black, were long and sinewy. I released the guilt upwards from my body to the sky where God took it from me. The guilt was caused by years of not being true to myself and not taking care of myself. The guilt was from years of pleasing others above true self and listening to the critical voice in my head.

There's some anger between my rib cage at the top of my stomach. It's from expecting others to take care of me when it's really myself I am angry at. I want others to give me the attention and love I don't give myself. That is not the case any longer.

True healing from within begins to take place after treatments. Until the treatments are over, the cancer patient is fighting a battle with fatigue, nausea, and fear every day. Only when my treatments were over, and I felt I was beginning to get my life back, did I really find the energy to go within and ask myself some hard questions. This is part of the recovery process. The ongoing, daily battle for strength to recover also is part of the process.

A good rule of thumb is a month of recovery for every month of treatment. This means if your friend was in chemotherapy and/or radiation for eight months, it may take eight more months for your friend to recover from the effects of those treatments. It doesn't end quickly. No matter what kind of treatments your friend has been through, the road to recovery from cancer is a long one.

My doctor told me the highest percentage of recurrence for Hodgkin's is within the first year. Fast-growing cancers (e.g., testicular cancer) might recur sooner than this, while slow-growing cancers (e.g., breast cancer) may take longer. The percentage of recurrence decreases each year until year five, ten or fifteen. After this, the risk of cancer is the same as for everyone else—one in three.

For at least the next five years, your friend will be having continual cancer check-ups. Learning to accept and adjust to these visits is another step in the recovery process. It's also a time for your friend to get acquainted with another routine of life. It means returning to work, seeing friends and acquaintances who may or may not know what your friend has been through, re-growing hair with its new texture and color, or living with an ostomy, mastectomy, or prosthesis. The list goes on. Being sensitive to all of the issues your friend is now facing will enable you to be supportive during this process.

Send Pamper Packages

Cancer treatments are very invasive. At times I had more needles, IVs, testing, cutting, and probing and poking than I felt I could take. It all seemed to reach a climax towards the end of my treatments.

Near the end of treatments is a good time to send a pamper package filled with relaxing, gentle, kind things for your friend. You can include several things already mentioned in the previous chapters, such as books, prayers, scriptures, meditations, or relaxation tapes. You might include aromatherapy bath oils, loofah sponges, candles, and certificates for massage (full body only if there are no traces of cancer remaining; hand and foot, otherwise). Other gift ideas include herbal teas, stuffed animals, and toys.

Try to give gifts that are appropriate for your friend. It is difficult to relax in a bath, for example, if you have pic lines—tubes used to administer the chemotherapy drugs—in your arms. Certain scents can trigger nausea in many cancer patients. But regardless of what you choose, the goal is to help your friend relax, feel good about themselves, and brighten his or her day.

Send Flowers

After treatments were completed was a time that I really appreciated getting flowers. A friend sent me a big beautiful vase of fresh-cut flowers, congratulating me on completing treatments. Sending flowers in celebration is a thoughtful expression of joy.

Have a Party

If your friend enjoys social gatherings, throw a celebration party. There's nothing better to celebrate than the completion of treatments. A party is an especially good idea if your friend has had to relocate to another city during the course of treatments. You can make the party a combination welcome-home and celebration party.

Plan a Trip

When your friend feels strong enough, plan a trip together. One friend used her frequent flyer miles to fly Jim and me to a family vacation home in

Maine for a celebration getaway. That was a little more extravagant than most people can do but, needless to say, we really enjoyed it.

Another friend flew Riley and me to her home in Texas so I could rest and Riley could play with her children. Yet another friend volunteered to watch Riley for a few days while Jim and I went to Santa Fe for our own celebration. All these were thoughtful gifts and gave my family and me a chance to get out of the house, change our environment, and celebrate my healing.

Encourage Rest

Although there's a great relief mentally and emotionally, your friend is physically at his or her weakest point when treatments end. Understand the need for rest—for a lot of it. Encourage your friend to rest.

Support Checkup Appointments

Follow-up appointments begin at two-week intervals and gradually extend to every six months. Your friend will be going for cancer checks regularly for life. These doctor visits are extremely anxious times. Remember to support your friend with phone calls or cards, especially during the first year. The highest percentage of recurrence happens during this time.

STILL NEEDED . . .

Housecleaning, lawn care, child care, gift certificates, money, cards, and phone calls are all still needed at this time and for the months ahead. Often, well-intentioned friends assume that because treatment is over and the cancer is in remission, everything is back to normal. It takes months to regain strength, and the fear of recurrence is always in the back of the mind, especially for the first year. Any of these thoughtful deeds will be appreciated, and will help your friend to know you are still there through the recovery process, too.

THINGS *NOT* TO DO:

1. *Don't assume when treatments are over your friend will be feeling back to normal.* It takes months or years for full recovery.

2. *Don't assume that the whole ordeal ends with treatments.* This is a tense period. Your friend must wait to see whether the cancer is completely gone or if it will return. Be sensitive to your friend's tests and doctor visits.

Everything in life that we really accept undergoes a change.[6]

—*Katherine Mansfield*

Chapter 7
Life Has Changed: Understanding Your "New" Friend

Cancer teaches you to live. I remember going to the chemotherapy room at the Cancer Center in Denver and being in awe at what I saw and by those I met. I walked away from that room, many times, inspired by the courage of the human spirit. They were fighting cancer and AIDS, and all with dignity, hope, and a sense of humor. It began to transform me. I knew I had choices each and every day of my life. I could learn and grow and live each day, or I could roll over and be a victim. After hearing the stories of others, I learned that what I faced seemed surmountable. It put my problems in perspective. I liked that! They were more manageable there.

I began to know, just as others who have gone before me, that life is a gift. And when I say know, I don't mean in the mind. I mean in the heart, where there is a true knowing. This opened me up to everything. I began to accept the love that was being given to me by my family and friends.

I credit my family for loving me so much and demonstrating their love so openly. Through their love, I began to see what unconditional love really is—that I, too, must love myself and others that way.

Cancer was the beginning of a new life-path for me, one that I am still on today. I haven't arrived, and I know I never will—no one ever does. But along that path, I have found a clarity in seeing the sacred in the everyday. I have changed in ways that are noticeable and in ways that cannot be seen.

Your friend has changed, too. If you've been alongside throughout this battle, you also have changed. Helping your friend through this difficult time can be one of the best experiences of your life, if you will embrace it, learn from it, grow from it. Talk to your friend about it. Ask him what he has learned. Ask him how cancer has changed his life.

My family and close friends talk to me about the changes cancer brought about in me, and that experience continues to bring us closer still. There are others who, for reasons of their own (mostly fear, I believe), have backed away from our friendship. This can be difficult to experience. But it is a reality that can occur with cancer and, more often, with change.

Have the courage, just as your friend has, to let cancer change your life. If your friend is still feeling anger and bitterness, help him to find the good that has come from the experience. In doing so, you'll find the good yourself. "One can never change the past, only the hold it has on you," writer Merle Shain reminds us, "and while nothing in your life is reversible, you can reverse it nevertheless."

Again, the best way to understand your new friend is to talk to her. It's hard for us to think of cancer as "good fortune," yet that's how most people who have survived see it. You don't have to look hard to find the courage, love, and gratitude all of us have found. Here are some words from people who've been there:

> *We go around thinking that real life is about adding a rec room to the basement, but it is not about real life. Cancer is real life. When you accept cancer, it is as if new systems within the organism automatically open—like oxygen masks and flotation systems that automatically drop in your lap on a 747 in an emergency. When you walk the earth on borrowed time,*

each day on the calendar is a beloved friend you know for only a short time.

—Judith Hooper, *Minding the Body: Women Writers on Body and Soul*

I have learned compassion. I now know that in the spectrum of time, all humans are working toward an ultimate goal. I have an inner sense of peace that was not there before. Nothing really matters but those truths that exist in one's own heart. You need only look deeply to find them.

—Mary Helen Brindell, *Chicken Soup for the Surviving Soul*

When I look back over the past four years and see all I've learned from other people who have suffered, all I've experienced of other people's love, all God has shown me of his mercy and comfort, all the encouragement my small measure of suffering has given to others, I think: If I'd have continued on as a ballplayer and missed that, now that would have been a tragedy.

—Dave Dravecky, *When You Can't Come Back*

> *Now, with a new attitude, a new spirit, a new life, I will place no unwarranted stress on this holy crucible of life that is my body on this earth. This is the pledge I make to myself. Never again will I let anything, or anyone, drag me down into suffering. Each day is too sacred to waste.*
>
> —Angela Passidomo Trafford, *The Heroic Path*

Journal Entry October 18, 1996 (one year after my diagnosis)

I guess it is so true that the body always remembers. I had a hard time sleeping last night. Try as I did, I could not release or shake this feeling in my chest. Or maybe my mind was hanging onto it because I saw it released so often but I still felt it . . . It was as if my body and mind were returning to the feelings of a year ago. Why? I feel like more answers will be revealed to me but I don't know now.

I felt like a storm was taking place inside of me last night, and I could not see clearly to understand much about it. I still feel a bit numb and blank this morning. So how do I love and support myself through this? Affirmations, prayer, and slowly changing my perspective. I do have mastery over fear and guilt. By accepting them I am then able to release them. But there is a part of me that questions all I'm really feeling. Fear, guilt, and what else? A fear that everything hasn't really changed from a year ago? No, just a fear of remembering what lay ahead for me one year ago today. That is my fear. What is my guilt? Getting cancer in the first place? Not taking care of myself well enough to prevent cancer? But yet, cancer has changed my life for the better. So is that the struggle or storm clouds that were clashing inside of me? Yes, that is it. The biggest challenge and the greatest suffering of my life have changed my life for the better . . .

Well, the tears just came. I feel such relief at where I am this year compared to last. It has been building inside of me and as I released it, they were tears of relief and gratitude. Gratitude that I'm sitting here looking at the mountains, the birds, the sky, and I am alive. How I love this earth and everything in it. How much we take for granted every single day of our lives . . . It is only through love of ourselves, others, and seeing every living creature as sacred that we understand how sacred and important our life is, too.

Why is it that some of us never learn that—and others must face death to see it so clearly? We are truly individuals with our own wills or we would all see it immediately. But we exercise our own will, combined with experiences and conditioning of our lives to keep us confused and searching and guiding ourselves.

I look at Riley and know she was sent to me to help with my battle. She alone was my biggest motivation for fighting. But there are so many more reasons I see around me today. I want to live so much for the joy and the beauty of this world. That joy and beauty is in me—I can see it now—and it will be with me always.

I heard a story several months ago, and it connected to a part of me, although I knew I didn't fully understand it. In it a teacher who was talking to a student said, "The difference between you and me is that you see yourself in the universe, [and] I see the universe in me."

It has taken me months—almost a year—but I'm beginning to understand that statement. I'm so thankful for the transformation that began taking place one year ago. I've changed and grown more during the past year than in all my life before that, I feel. That may not be totally true but it is the most profound change I have ever felt because it is more of an understanding of life, love, and God. It means living my life in faith, not in knowing all of the answers.

I used to look for answers all around me and push until I found one. Now, I trust the information I need to know will be revealed to me, and that my life is truly in higher hands. I'm glad about that, as God's divine plan is far more enlightened than my earthly vision. Now I feel that God's will is my will, as I have let go of my own.

But that doesn't mean I don't love and support myself, because I do. It's just different. It comes from love. I found that love through cancer and through the love that was shown to me by God, friends, and family. I've found the infinite well of love that is within me and was there all along. Through the faith and beliefs that others showed in me, I found it in myself. What a glorious journey I have been on and what excitement I have to look forward to. Thank you God, thank you family, thank you friends, for giving me my life.

True health is the strength to live, the strength to suffer,and the strength to die.[7]

—Jürgen Moltmann

Chapter 8
Saying Good-Bye

By the grace of God, I now accept death as a natural certainty of life. Although the medical community has recently pronounced me "cured" from Hodgkin's Disease, and many people do survive cancer, death is a very real part of the disease. Every cancer patient must face it.

Despite all the efforts of family, friends, and medical staff, some cancer does not respond to treatments. Sometimes a cancer patient just gets tired of the battle.

Sometimes cancer wins—or does it? Through Jesus Christ, we are offered hope, even in death. That hope is the only true peace I have found when a loved one is dying.

Supporting a friend who is dying of cancer demands incredible strength. From those with experience, I have collected some suggestions for being supportive. I hope they will be of comfort to both you and your friend.

Be Honest

In a study done more than 20 years ago, Dr. Elisabeth Kübler-Ross discovered that the dying know their futures and often feel isolated by their refusal of others to discuss death with them. Be completely honest with your friend—and with yourself. Talk openly about your fears, your worries, the future, as well as your anger.

Be willing to confront and accept all the feelings you discuss with your friend. Your openness and honesty will benefit both of you, easing pain and bringing you both closer together.

Include Your Friend

Death is painful, and sometimes people try to protect themselves from the pain by avoiding the one who is dying. Talk to your friend when in the room together. Don't assume he or she can't hear you. Talk to others outside of the room when privacy is needed.

Reminisce

Start talking to your friend or loved one. Talk to him or her about friends, family members, important or daily events. Reminisce about the past. Remember old times together. Share favorite memories.

In *Widowed* (New York: Ballantine Books, 1990), Dr. Joyce Brothers describes her last hours with her husband like this:

> I talked for hours. I talked about the silly things, the good things, the times that I had cherished, about everything that had been important to me in our life together. I held his hand and poured my heart out. I told him over and over how much I loved him and how happy he had always made me.

There is wisdom in her words. Go through photo albums together, watch home movies, and bring out cherished keepsakes shared together. Let your friend know that his or her life meant something, was precious.

Make Good Memories

In my work with our cancer support outreach, I have found that the dying hold onto their memories. Make these last memories good ones. Spend time together. Find out what unfinished business might haunt them and help them find resolve and serenity.

As is common, my grandfather needed to know his sins were forgiven and that he was going to heaven. He also wanted to know that my grandmother was there. We called the pastor of his church who came over and spent two days with my grandfather.

If your friend has a final wish in this life, try to make it happen. Help them to leave this world with a feeling that all is complete.

Continue to Pray

Never stop asking for God's assistance. No matter what the diagnosis, continue to pray for healing. It comes in many forms.

Hospital or Hospice

Often care of a cancer patient becomes too much for friends and family to perform. Seek help from the medical community on which type of clinical care would be best for your friend. Ask your friend what type of care he or she would like to receive.

There are usually three options based on the medical needs of your friend. One is full-time hospital care. Another is full-time care at a hospice facility (a hospice is similar to a hospital but with more room). The third type of care is hospice care in the home. Regardless of what choice is made, making the decision early is generally a good idea.

Bring Food to the Family

In cases where death seems inevitable, family often gathers to say good-bye. Bringing food to the family enables them to focus on more important matters. I've often heard much appreciation for this simple gesture.

The following suggestions might be helpful if you plan to bring food to a family at a hospital or hospice: bring complete meals in disposable containers along with drinks, silverware, napkins, etc.

Run Errands

Getting out can become very difficult for the caregiver. Leaving their loved one, even for a short period of time, may make them anxious.

Offer to run errands for them. Ask for their grocery list and go to the store for them. If the patient and caregiver are open to it, offer to sit with him or her while the caregiver takes a much needed break. (However, be sensitive. A cancer patient's appearance changes dramatically over the course of the disease. I know of several patients who will only allow certain people to see them.)

Review Will and Trusts

Obviously, legal matters can only be done by those with experience, but it is a much-needed service. My husband's cousin is an attorney. He immediately offered to set up a living will.

Even if your friend has already completed the will, trust, and power of attorney, it is a good idea to have it reviewed. I've heard of cases where the family thought all this had been taken care of only to find it incomplete after the death of their loved one.

Seek and Accept Support for Yourself

A cancer battle can be long and painful, whether a cure is found or not. Learn to care for yourself as you learn to care for your friend. Share the many responsibilities between friends and family.

Additionally, you might want to seek the help of professionals such as ministers, therapists, support groups, and hospital social workers. These people will also be able to direct you to professional organizations both nationally and in your local area. Don't try to play all the roles yourself. You will need support long after death comes.

Good-bye is something we say easily everyday, but it can send us reeling when it comes time to say it for the last time to someone we love. I don't have an easy answer for you. My hope and prayer is that your journey together has led you to find the blessings that are hidden in the pain of cancer. Don't misunderstand me, I do not believe cancer is a blessing, but I do know there are blessings to be found along the way.

He will wipe away every tear from their eyes. There will be no more death or mourning or crying or pain, for the old order of things has passed away. He who was seated on the throne said, "I am making everything new!"

—Revelation 21:4-5

Acknowledgments

My story is about the unconditional love and support that surrounded me and lifted me up, even when I was unable to lift myself. It is about finding the strength to heal your life.

Perhaps more specifically, this book is about how my family and friends, through their gifts, prayers, and thoughtful deeds, showed me the true meaning of love. They were a very big reason for my successful recovery from cancer. This book is dedicated to them.

My Family

Jim . . . for loving me in sickness and in health. I am grateful to have you as my life-partner. Together forever.

Riley . . . for being the best daily dose of medicine I had. You are God's special gift.

Dad . . . you are my hero. Your love and dedication have given rise to the love within me. Thank you for making sure I was never alone.

Mother . . . you have given me a true role model for the word mother. Thank you.

Paula . . . for your nurturing and giving soul. You bring me comfort and love. Sisters are forever.

Tricia . . . for your spiritual guidance, friendship, and love for me. I love you, too!

Perry . . . for keeping me company when I needed it most and your deep convictions of recovery.

Jim's family . . . for supporting us.

My Friends

Karen . . . for being with me in person, on the phone, and always in spirit.

Diane . . . for your tireless devotion to seeing me through this. You were truly there for me.

Sabra . . . whose words appear often in this book. You are a courageous, beautiful soul who showed me how to find my way as only a fellow cancer warrior could. Thank you for sharing your beliefs, ideas, and experiences.

DeDe . . . for your time and gifts given in loving support.

Katie . . . for reaching out to us and giving Riley a loving, fun home to visit. You came for a reason, and we were blessed.

Linda . . . for doing whatever needed to be done without hesitation and for just being my friend.

And to the countless others who were truly an inspiration to us—thank you.

For Further Reading

Books that I found helpful and their descriptions follow below:

Medical Guides

A Medical and Spiritual Guide to Living with Cancer by William A. Fintel, M.D., and Gerald R. McDermott, Ph.D. This comprehensive book helps answer medical and spiritual questions about cancer and the role it plays in the lives of patients and their families.

Everyone's Guide to Cancer Therapy by Malin Dollinger, M.D., Ernest H. Rosenbaum, M.D., and Greg Cable. This is an easy-to-read book on how cancer is diagnosed, treated, and managed day to day.

Cancer Therapy: The Independent Consumer's Guide to Non-Toxic Treatment and Prevention by Ralph W. Moss, Ph.D. This book details nearly 100 non-toxic or less toxic treatments for cancer.

When Cancer Comes by Don Hawkins, Daniel L. Koppersmith, M.D., and Ginger Koppersmith. Using experience of professionals in the medical, psychological, and spiritual battlefronts, this book advises you to take aggressive action in fighting cancer and shows you how to do it.

Nutrition and Cancer

Beating Cancer with Nutrition by Patrick Quillan, Ph.D., R.D., C.N.S., with Noreen Quillan. This book contains "clinically proven strategies to dramatically improve your quality and quantity of life and chances for a complete remission" (Nutrition Times Press). Its strategies can be used in conjunction with traditional treatments.

Nutrition, The Cancer Answer by Maureen Kennedy Salaman. Salaman discusses how cancer can be prevented and even reversed through nutrition.

Personal Success Stories

A Cancer Battle Plan by Anne E. Frahm with David J. Frahm. This book tells how Anne fought and reversed Stage-IV breast cancer. It provides "six strategies for beating cancer, including resource lists and a complete nutrition battle plan" (Putnam).

Anatomy of an Illness as Perceived by the Patient by Norman Cousins. This book recounts how Norman "laughed" his way back to health and demonstrates the power of using the mind and body together to overcome illness.

Chicken Soup for the Surviving Soul by Jack Canfield, Mark Victor Hansen, Patty Aubrey and Nancy Mitchell, R.N. The book contains stories of inspiration and courage from survivors.

50 Essential Things to Do When the Doctor Says It's Cancer by Greg Anderson. Diagnosed with lung cancer and given thirty days to live, this cancer survivor shares how he and other patients survived their illness.

The Cancer Conqueror: An Incredible Journey to Wellness by Greg Anderson. This is a powerful story of how one man conquered what doctors thought to be terminal cancer.

The Heroic Path by Angela Passidomo Trafford. This book chronicles one woman's journey from two diagnoses of breast cancer to self-healing.

When You Can't Come Back by Dave and Jan Dravecky. This is an inspirational story of the author, once an All-Star pitcher, who lost his arm to cancer, and how he and his wife turned adversity into strength and hope for themselves and others.

Spiritual and Emotional Meditations

Do Not Lose Heart by Dave and Jan Dravecky. Based on 2 Corinthians 4:16-18, this book shares meditations of encouragement and comfort to those who suffer.

Everyday Strength: A Cancer Patient's Guide to Spiritual Survival by Randy Becton. This is a book of daily meditations and prayers written by a cancer survivor.

Love, Medicine and Miracles: Lessons Learned About Self-Healing from a Surgeon's Experience With Exceptional Patients by Bernie S. Siegel, M.D. This book shows how unconditional love is the most powerful stimulant to the immune system.

Readings for Meditation and Reflection by C. S. Lewis. "Gathered from his mass of published work, this book offers probing insights, passionate arguments, and provocative questions about God, love, life, and death" (HarperCollins).

The Problem of Pain by C. S. Lewis. Lewis offers intellectual answers to the critical question, "If God is both omnipotent and good, how can we explain the pain and suffering that people experience daily?" (Touchstone Books).

Readings and Prayers

The following readings and prayers are a few of my favorites:

Hope is the thing with feathers
That perches in the soul,
And sings the tune without the words,
And never stops at all.[8]

—Emily Dickinson

Do not look forward to the changes and chances of this life in fear. Rather look at them with full hope that as they arise, God, whose you are, will deliver you out of them. He has kept you hitherto; do you but hold fast to His dear hand, and He will lead you safely through all things; and when you cannot stand, He will bear you in His arms.[9]

—Saint Francis de Sales

It is God who arms me with strength and makes my way perfect.

—2 Samuel 22:33

Peace I leave with you; my peace I give you. I do not give to you as the world gives. Do not let your hearts be troubled and do not be afraid.

—John 14:27

Therefore, we do not lose heart. Though outwardly we are wasting away, yet inwardly we are being renewed day by day. For our light and momentary troubles are achieving for us an eternal glory that far outweighs them all. So we fix our eyes on not what is seen, but on what is unseen. For what is seen is temporary, but what is unseen is eternal.

—2 Corinthians 4:16-18

My grace is sufficient for thee; for my strength is made perfect in weakness.

—2 Corinthians 12:9

Do not be anxious about anything, but in everything, by prayer and petition, with Thanksgiving, present your requests to God.

—Philippians 4:6

Dear Lord,

Sometimes I wish suffering weren't a part of the landscape of life. There is so much uncertainty, so many questions, and so few answers, that at times I do all I can to avoid suffering. But now I find myself smack dab in the middle of it and there seems to be nowhere to turn, except to you.

I thank you, Lord, that the Bible, your Word, gives such incredible comfort in the midst of storms like this. Help me, Lord, to hold on to those words of encouragement so that I may have the strength I need to endure this journey.

I am so grateful for the many examples in your Word of men and women who have suffered. I am grateful not only for them but also for those who are suffering all around me yet encourage me not to lose heart. Most important of all to me is that your Son, Jesus, knew suffering more deeply than any of us . . . and yet he did not lose heart. Through his life you have given me the strength to cope in the midst of the storm!

You know, Lord, I'd like to say one more thing before I finish. Thanks for putting the warning signs up there that tells us we will suffer, that suffering is a part of life in this fallen world. But thanks also for allowing us—for allowing me—the freedom to express my fears about the future. For only when I do so am I able to realize my dependence upon the One who understands my suffering better than anyone. Because he did not lose heart when he suffered, I, too, can find the strength to live courageously in my own difficult circumstances. Amen.[10]

—Dave Dravecky

Dear God,

My body is sick and I am scared, so weak, so sad. Please heal me, Lord. Whatever the words I am supposed to say, whatever the thoughts that would set me free, I am willing to have them shine into my mind. For I wish to be released. Please give me a miracle. Please give me hope. Please give me peace. Lift me up beyond the regions of my pain and despair.

Prepare each cell to be born anew into health and happiness, peace and love. For You are the power, not this sickness. You are the truth, not this illusion. You are my salvation, not the doctor.

I am willing to rise, to let go all false thinking, to release this false condition. For this is not freedom, and I wish to be free. This is not peaceful, and I desire peace. This is not Your will for me, that I would suffer or feel pain.

I accept Your will for me, I accept Your healing, I accept Your love. Please, dear God, help me. Take me home. Amen.[11]

—Marianne Williamson

The Lord is my light and my salvation—whom shall I fear? The Lord is the stronghold of my life—of whom shall I be afraid? . . . I am still confident of this: I will see the goodness of the Lord in the land of the living. Wait for the Lord; be strong and take heart and wait for the Lord.

—Psalm 27:1-2, 13-14

Hear my cry, O God; listen to my prayer. From the ends of the earth I call to you, I call as my heart grows faint; lead me to the rock that is higher than I. For you have been my refuge, a strong tower against the foe. I long to dwell in your tent forever and take refuge in the shelter of your wings.

—Psalm 61:1-4

I Said A Prayer for You Today

I said a prayer for you today and know God
must have heard—
I felt the answer in my heart although he spoke
no word!
I didn't ask for wealth or fame (I knew you
wouldn't mind)—
I asked Him to send treasures of a far more lasting
kind!
I asked that He'd be near you at the start of each
new day
To grant you health and blessings and friends to
share your way!
I asked for happiness for you in all things great
and small—
But it was for His loving care I prayed the most
of all!

—Author Unknown

The prayers that follow may be prayed for or with a friend:

God, you gave my friend and me life.
Cancer has turned our lives upside
down. We ask you for strength to
struggle with it physically, mentally,
and spiritually. We ask that you care
for our loved ones in your special way,
and let us use this experience for
something good in our lives. Be very
close to us. Amen.[12]

—Randy Becton

Father, I pray, God that you will give
my friend Your presence, Your strength.
Give the ability to trust. When all emotions
doubt, give my friend that ability to hang on.
Restore health. This I ask for my friend
from you, My God, if it can be your will.[13]

—Randy Becton

May the Light shine on all your day.
It is there, despite illness, defeat, and tears.
It is eternal.[14]

—Harvey Stower

Notes

1. Bernie S. Siegel, *Love, Medicine and Miracles* (New York: Harper and Row, 1986), ix.

2. Mary Dawson Hughes, *The Little Book of "Thank You's"* (Kansas City, Mo.: Hallmark Cards, Inc., 1990).

3. Charles Haddon Spurgeon, as quoted in *Who Said That?: More Than 2,500 Usable Quotes and Illustrations*, compiled by George Sweeting (Chicago: Moody Press, 1995).

4. St. Teresa of Avila (1515–1582), as quoted in *Simple Abundance*, by Sarah Ban Breathnach (New York: Warner Books, 1995)

5. Ralph Waldo Emerson (1803–1882), source unknown.

6. Katherine Mansfield (1888-1923), source unknown.

7. Jürgen Moltmann, as quoted in *Where Is God When It Hurts*, by Philip Yancey (Grand Rapids, Mich.: Zondervan Publishing House, 1990).

8. Emily Dickinson (1830–1886). *Complete Poems of Emily Dickinson*, ed. Thomas H. Johnson (Boston: Little Brown, 1960).

9. St. Francis de Sales (1567–1622), source unknown.

10. Dave and Jan Dravecky, with Steve Halliday, *Do Not Lose Heart* (Grand Rapids, Mich.: Zondervan Publishing House, 1988), 35–36. Copyright © 1998 David and Janice Dravecky. Used by permission of Zondervan Publishing House.

11. Marianne Williamson, *Illuminata: A Return to Prayer* (New York: Riverhead Books, 1995). Copyright © 1994 by Marianne Williamson. Used by permission of Random House, Inc.

12. and 13. Randy Becton, *Everyday Strength: A Cancer Patient's Guide to Spiritual Survival* (Grand Rapids, Mich.: Baker Book House, 1989). Copyright © 1989 Randy Becton. Used by permission of Baker Book House Company.

14. Harvey Stower, *All Will Be Well: A Gathering of Healing Prayers*, ed. Lyn Klug (Minneapolis: Augsburg, 1998), 29. Copyright © Harvey Stower. Used by permission.

Dear Reader:

You have just read about the power of support in caring for a friend or loved one. Do you have stories about the support and encouragement you received or gave during an encounter with cancer? Send your stories of how cancer survivors were helped to:

Survivor Support Stories
P.O. Box 26344
Colorado Springs, CO
80936-6344

All stories will remain confidential.